The White House

The White House

Patricia Ryon Quiri

Franklin Watts

A DIVISION OF GROLIER PUBLISHING

NEW YORK   LONDON   HONG KONG   SYDNEY
DANBURY, CONNECTICUT

For my sisters Judy McGrath
and Cathy Todd, and my brother
Fred Ryon, with love.

Cover photographs copyright ©: Library of Congress: top left, top center; Bettmann: top right; The White House: bottom left; Folio Inc.: bottom right (Lelia Hendren)

Photographs copyright ©: Folio Inc.: p. 2 (Robert C. Shafer); Library of Congress: pp. 8, 12 bottom right, 17(all), 23, 33, 44; North Wind Picture Archives: p. 10; The Historical Society of Washington, D.C.: pp. 12 top left, 14 top right, 16; The Bettmann Archive: pp. 14 bottom, 22, 31, 43, 47, 52; Reuters/Bettman: p. 56; Jay Mallin, Library of Congress: p. 19 (both); Anne S. K. Brown Military College, Brown University Library: p. 20; White House Historical Association: pp. 24, 26, 27, 28, 30, 35; John Fitzgerald Kennedy Library: p. 37; The White House: p. 39; AP/Wide World Photos: p. 40; Photri: pp. 48 (Lani Novak Howe), 55; Courtesy Gerald R. Ford Library: p. 51.

Library of Congress Cataloging-in-Publication Data

Quiri, Patricia Ryon.
    The White House / Patricia Ryon Quiri.
      p. cm. — (A First book)
    Includes bibliographical references and index.
    ISBN 0-531-20221-6
    1. White House (Washington, D.C.)—Juvenile literature. 2. Presidents—United States—Juvenile literature. 3. Washington (D.C.)—Buildings, structures, etc.—Juvenile literature.
    I. Title. II. Series.
    F204.W5Q57 1996
    975.3—dc20
                                            95-44444
                                          CIP AC

Contents

The White House

IN 1789, GEORGE WASHINGTON WAS INAUGURATED IN THE TEMPORARY
CAPITAL OF THE UNITED STATES — NEW YORK CITY.

Chapter One

CHOOSING A SITE FOR THE FEDERAL CITY

When George Washington was inaugurated president of the United States of America in 1789, New York City was the new country's temporary capital. When it came time to establish a permanent federal city, the leaders of the young nation disagreed over where the capital city would be. Fearing a southern capital would influence government, Northerners wanted the capital to remain in their part of the country. Similar concerns caused the Southerners to argue for moving the capital to the South.

There were good reasons for wanting the new capital city nearby. Building a new federal city meant the creation of jobs, a boom in the local economy, and a rise in the value of local property. And citizens close to the capital would have better access to, and perhaps more control over, government officials than other citizens.

Other factors that came into consideration in choosing a place for the federal city included the site's weather and climate, types of transportation, condition of the soil, cost of building materials, sources of energy, and access to the Atlantic Ocean and western territories. Much atten-

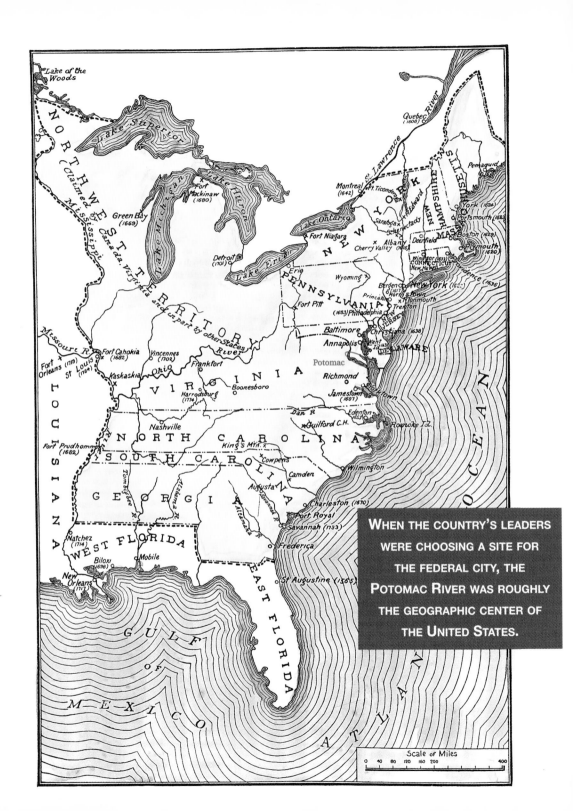

When the country's leaders were choosing a site for the federal city, the Potomac River was roughly the geographic center of the United States.

tion was given to choosing a central location. Northerners and Southerners could not even agree on where the central point of the country was located. When Northerners spoke of centrality, they considered the distribution of the population, but to Southerners, centrality was the center of territory. At that time, the geographic center of the United States was the Potomac River.

Thanks to two political opponents, the secretary of the treasury, Alexander Hamilton, and the secretary of state, Thomas Jefferson, an agreement about the headquarters of the new capital was reached. Because the new government had to establish national credit, Hamilton wanted the federal government to take over the individual states' war debts. If Jefferson could get the southern states to agree to this condition, Hamilton would try to convince the northern states to allow a capital site by the Potomac River. After seven long years of debate, Congress finally passed a bill stating that the location of the new capital city would be along the banks of the Potomac River.

In fall 1790, the temporary capital was moved from New York City to Philadelphia, Pennsylvania. The government operated there for ten years while the new capital city was being built.

President George Washington chose the exact site for the new federal city. A former land surveyor, Washington had a lot of experience. Maryland and Virginia each

ALEXANDER HAMILTON

THOMAS JEFFERSON

offered land on the banks of the Potomac River to make up a 10-mile square, or a plot of 100 square miles (259 sq km), in which to construct the city. In the end, only the land given by Maryland was used and Virginia was given back its portion in 1847. Present-day Washington, D.C., is 69 square miles (179 sq km).

George Washington chose a spot with an outstanding view for the president's house, and the White House stands there today. In those days, the young country was nicknamed "Columbia," in honor of Christopher Columbus. As a district, not a state, the area was called the District of Columbia, or "D.C." The federal city itself would be named for George Washington, which is how the capital of the United States got its name—Washington, D.C.

PIERRE-CHARLES L'ENFANT

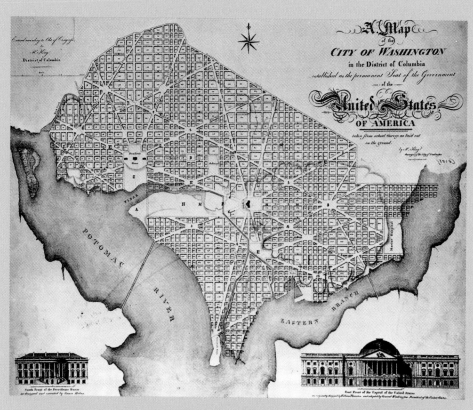

L'ENFANT'S PLAN FOR WASHINGTON, D.C., A GRID OF STREETS

WITH AVENUES RUNNING DIAGONALLY

Chapter Two

PLANNING THE NEW CAPITAL

George Washington hired an architect, Pierre-Charles L'Enfant, to design the new federal city. L'Enfant was a Frenchman who had fought in the American Revolutionary War under Washington. Raised in Versailles, France, L'Enfant wanted to create a capital city in the United States to equal a magnificent European city. He also wanted to build a fabulous official residence for the president of the United States. He planned streets, buildings, and parks in addition to the "Presidential Palace."

George Washington and most other Americans, however, did not want anything fancy. They also didn't want to call the president's house a palace. Back then, the United States of America had just begun to be a democratic country, not a country with a monarchy, like England, ruled by kings and queens. Americans had fought hard for their independence from England and wanted to do things their own way.

Because L'Enfant was uncompromising, and his grand plans were much more than the new country could afford, he was fired from the job of designing the federal city and the so-called President's House. Much to his fury,

BENJAMIN BANNEKER

L'Enfant's designs were remembered by a brilliant African-American mathematician and writer, Benjamin Banneker, who used them as a guide for later construction of the city.

Soon, the Board of Federal Commissioners, appointed by Congress, sought architectural plans for the President's House. In 1792, Thomas Jefferson wrote an advertisement for designs in the country's leading newspapers. A cash prize of $500 or a gold medal worth the same would be awarded to the person whose plans the commissioners accepted. Jefferson himself submitted a design, under a different name, but did not win the contest. A man by the name of James Hoban, born in 1762 in Callan, Ireland, won the job and chose the gold medal as his prize.

Hoban worked with George Washington on the details of the President's House. They changed the original design from three to two main stories. The house was to be impressive and graceful, made of stone instead of wood or brick, with elegant lawns and gardens surrounding it. Although it is difficult to imagine now, the land on which this house was to be built was swampy and filled with trees. Wild animals, including bears and deer, lived on

JAMES HOBAN

JAMES HOBAN'S ORIGINAL DESIGN
FOR THE WHITE HOUSE

A REJECTED DRAWING OF
THE PRESIDENT'S HOUSE
THOUGHT TO BE THE WORK
OF THOMAS JEFFERSON

the property. In those days there was no machinery. Slaves removed the trees with their bare hands.

On October 13, 1792, the first cornerstone of the President's House was laid in the southwest corner. Everyone in Washington gathered for the historic event. An inscribed brass plate was laid underneath the cornerstone. It read:

This first stone of the President's House was laid the 13th day of October 1792, and in the seventeenth year of the independence of the United States of America
George Washington, President
Thomas Johnson
Doctor Stewart
Daniel Carroll
Commissioners
James Hoban, Architect
Collen Williamson, Master Mason
Vivat Republica

["Long Live the Republic"]

To this day, this brass plate has never been found.

Finally, in November 1800, the President's House was ready for its first tenants—John Adams, the second president of the United States, and his wife, Abigail. (George Washington's term of office was 1789–97 and he died on December 14, 1799.)

Beginning with John Adams, the House was open to the public. It was called either the President's House, the

JOHN AND ABIGAIL ADAMS,
THE WHITE HOUSE'S FIRST TENANTS

Executive Mansion, or the President's Palace. Everyone was anxious to see the new, unfinished house. Before its completion, streams of people visited the house, creating great confusion. The commissioners of the district finally announced that all visitors required a written pass to enter. Since it was built, the White House has remained open to the public at certain times. It is the only home of any world leader that regularly gives tours.

Two years after the first shots of the War of 1812 were fired,
British troops invaded the federal city.

Chapter Three

A HOUSE ON FIRE

On June 18, 1812, James Madison, the fourth U.S. president, signed a declaration of war against Great Britain for seizing American ships and blockading American harbors. This conflict, known as the War of 1812, was dubbed "Mr. Madison's War" by the president's foes. Two years later, in August 1814, the British stormed into the federal city and burned many of its public buildings, including the Capitol and the President's House.

Before the British invaded Washington, D.C., the president's wife, Dolley Madison, quickly packed the Declaration of Independence and the Constitution, along with the silver and some draperies. Before she fled the President's House, she insisted on taking down from the dining room the huge portrait of George Washington, painted by Gilbert Stuart. The picture frame was so heavy that it had been nailed to the wall. The first lady had one of her servants cut the picture out of the frame, gave it to two men from New York for safekeeping, and departed with her maid.

Hours later, the British stormed the capital city. Before they torched the President's House, the British officers sat down to a meal that had been set out for President

Madison. They also stole several items from the House. One hundred and twenty-five years later, a descendant of one soldier returned to the U.S. government a medicine cabinet believed to have belonged to James Madison.

The day after the British set Washington ablaze, a fierce hurricane swept the city. The fearful British ran to their ships to escape high winds and heavy rain. Two days later, Dolley Madison returned to the terrible destruction of the capital city. The President's House was a blackened shell. The outer stone walls still stood, but the inside was ruined.

James Hoban, the original White House architect, was hired to rebuild the President's House in 1815. He was paid $1,600 a year. The total cost of the reconstruction was about $300,000, which was what it had cost to build the President's House the first time. When the fifth U.S. president, James Monroe, and his family moved into the House in 1817, Congress granted $20,000 to furnish the bare house. Monroe used the money to purchase furni-

THE INTERIOR OF THE PRESIDENT'S HOUSE WAS DESTROYED BY
THE BRITISH DURING THEIR INVASION OF WASHINGTON, D.C.

ture from France. When another $30,000 was approved to spend a year later, Monroe spent most of the money on products made in the United States.

After the House was rebuilt, its gleaming white walls gave way to the popular but unofficial name "White House." The name did not become official until the turn of the century when Theodore Roosevelt ordered "White House" printed on his presidential stationery.

FORMAL RECEPTIONS TAKE PLACE IN THE BLUE ROOM, WHICH DISPLAYS
PRESIDENTIAL PORTRAITS. ON THE LEFT SIDE OF THE CENTER WINDOW IS
A PORTRAIT OF JAMES MADISON AND ON THE RIGHT IS THOMAS JEFFERSON.

Chapter Four

INSIDE THE WHITE HOUSE

*V*isitors to the White House enter on the Ground Floor corridor of the East Wing and proceed up the marble stairs to the First Floor, also known as the State Floor. They see the East Room, the Green Room, the Blue Room, the Red Room, and the State Dining Room. The furniture and antique collection in these rooms span the country's history. Tourists get a distinct sense of the past as they go from room to room. Paintings of U.S. presidents, first ladies, and their families are on display. No president ever removes these paintings or furnishings, because they belong to the White House and are all part of U.S. history.

THE BLUE ROOM

This room is oval and faces south. George Washington probably influenced James Hoban to design the Blue Room as an oval so that visitors of the president could sit in a semicircle. This floor plan made it easy to receive a circle of callers, which President Washington greatly enjoyed.

Formerly called the Drawing Room, the Blue Room was used as a reception room. It got its name during Martin Van Buren's administration (1837–41), when the room was decorated in shades of blue.

Since then, the room has been redecorated many times, but the blue theme has remained. The furniture that James Monroe bought from Paris after the 1814 White House fire was in the French Empire style. Seven of these chairs and a sofa are on display in the Blue Room today. Portraits of presidents John Adams, Thomas Jefferson, and Andrew Jackson are among the many that hang in this room.

The Blue Room today is a formal reception room where the president greets his guests. The oval Blue Room should not be confused with the Oval Office.

NAMED FOR THE DELICATE WATERED-GREEN SILK THAT COVERS ITS WALLS, THE GREEN ROOM IS USED FOR INFORMAL RECEPTIONS.

THE GREEN ROOM

This room is located to the east of the Blue Room. Decorated with furniture built by Duncan Phyfe, a celebrated Scottish-born cabinetmaker, it is used today for informal receptions. Over the years, the room has had many other uses. It served as a guest room for visitors of John Adams, as a dining room for Thomas Jefferson, and as a card room for friends of James Monroe. A portrait of Benjamin Franklin hangs on a wall of the Green Room. During James Monroe's administration (1817–25), the room was decorated in green, and the name and color have lasted.

THE RED ROOM

This room, previously known as the Yellow Drawing Room, is located on the west side of the Blue Room. Dolley Madison used to hold her famous Wednesday-night parties in this room. Politically influential, she entertained many people here, from her husband's friends to his enemies. The first lady was even known to share a little snuff in the Red Room with her husband's foes.

DECORATED IN CRIMSON AND GOLD, THE RED ROOM SERVES AS A SITTING ROOM.

During James Monroe's administration, the walls of the room were redecorated with red silk fabric flanked with gold trim, and since then it has been known as the Red Room. It is used as a parlor, or sitting room. A striking portrait of Martin Van Buren's daughter-in-law and hostess, Angelica Singleton Van Buren, done in 1842, is located above the mantel in the Red Room. The furniture in the room today dates back to 1810–30.

ELABORATE TABLE SETTINGS, FRESH FLOWERS, AND CANDLELIT CHANDELIERS ARE CUSTOMARY FOR BANQUETS IN THE STATE DINING ROOM.

THE STATE DINING ROOM

The large and impressive State Dining Room, glittering in gold and white, is located at the west end of the White House and faces south. The president can entertain up to 140 dinner guests here. The room was originally much smaller and was not used as a dining room. Over the years, it has served as the Cabinet Room, an office, and a drawing room. Abraham Lincoln's wife, Mary Todd, even set up a schoolroom in this room for sons Willie and Tad.

During Andrew Jackson's administration (1829–37), this room became the State Dining Room. Later, Theodore Roosevelt (who held office 1901–09) had a passion for hunting and displayed large animal trophies on the walls, including a huge head of a moose. These animal trophies have since been donated to the Smithsonian Institution, located in Washington, D.C. A portrait of Abraham Lincoln, executed by artist George P. A. Healy in 1869, now hangs above the fireplace. Beneath this portrait, inscribed on the mantel, are the words of the first president to live in the White House, second president John Adams. In a letter to his wife, Abigail, on his first night in the White House in November 1800, John Adams wrote: "I Pray Heaven to Bestow the Best of Blessings on This House, And All that shall Hereafter inhabit it. May None but Honest and Wise Men ever rule under This Roof."

The East Room

The largest in the White House, this room measures 79 feet (24 m) by nearly 37 feet (11 m). Guests are entertained after formal dinners in the East Room, named for its location on the east side of the White House. Dances, concerts, and special programs are put on in this great room. When John and Abigail Adams moved into the

THE LARGEST ROOM IN THE WHITE HOUSE, THE EAST ROOM
IS USED FOR BOTH SOMBER AND FESTIVE OCCASIONS.

White House in November 1800, the East Room was not yet finished, and the first lady hung her laundry in the large room. The East Room was not completed and furnished until 1829. Because many guests must fit into this room, it is sparsely furnished. Enormous and vacant, this room was perfect for Theodore Roosevelt's children when they wanted to roller skate.

Abraham Lincoln, the sixteenth president of the United States, was the first president whose body lay in state in the East Room. He was shot in Ford's Theater on April 14, 1865, by a man named John Wilkes Booth, who supported the South. The president died the next morning.

As a president who worked to abolish slavery, Lincoln had had many threats to his life over the issue. A forewarning of his death came to him in his sleep before the shooting at Ford's Theater. In a dream, Lincoln heard wailing sounds and followed the noise to the East Room. When he entered the room, he saw a catafalque, an elevated structure that holds a coffin during a state funeral. A body was in the coffin, and people stood crying around it. A soldier guarding the catafalque whispered to Lincoln, "The President . . . killed by an assassin." Tragically, the eerie dream came true two weeks later.

The funeral of William Henry Harrison, the first U.S. president to die in office, was also held in the East Room. Harrison was inaugurated on March 4, 1841. He was sixty-eight years old, and at that time, the oldest person to become president. After giving the longest inaugural speech in history on a bitter-cold day, Harrison died of pneumonia one month later.

Zachary Taylor died in office on July 9, 1850. His death was a result of heat exhaustion from a July 4 celebration. He had served only sixteen months in the White House.

James Garfield was the only U.S. president to die in office whose body did not lie in state in the East Room. Another victim of an assassin's bullet, he was shot on July 2, 1881, and eventually died of his wounds. Garfield's body was taken to the Capitol to lie in state in the Rotunda.

On September 14, 1901, William McKinley, twenty-fifth U.S. president, died as a result of gunshot wounds. Warren Harding became ill and died in office on August 2, 1923. Franklin D. Roosevelt, who served longest as president, twelve years, died on April 12, 1945. President John F. Kennedy, another victim of an assailant's bullet, was shot in Dallas, Texas, on November 22, 1963.

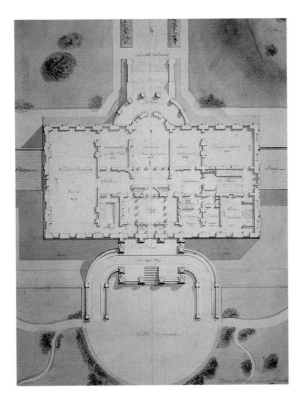

IN 1807, BENJAMIN HENRY LATROBE DESIGNED THIS PLAN FOR CHANGING THE FIRST STORY OF THE WHITE HOUSE AND ADDING PORTICOS.

NORTH AND SOUTH PORTICOS

At the end of the White House tour, visitors exit through the North Portico, which is the main entrance to the White House. This side of the house faces Pennsylvania Avenue, and has a square portico, or porch, which juts out and has columns. This feature was not part of the original House plan. Thomas

Jefferson asked architect Benjamin Henry Latrobe to prepare designs for a portico, which was completed later, in 1829. Because no picture-taking is allowed inside the building, visitors usually take their pictures here.

It was President James Monroe who had Latrobe and Hoban design a portico for the south entrance of the house. This porch, circular with large columns supporting it, was finished in 1824.

Second Floor of the White House

Very few people are ever allowed upstairs to the second and third floors of the White House. The second floor contains the first family's living areas: bedrooms, a family room, and a private kitchen for the president's family. There are also offices on this floor for the president's staff.

The Queens' Room, located on the second story, used to be called the Rose Guest Room. After five queens from different foreign countries stayed in this room, its name was changed. Relatives and close friends of the president, as well as visiting dignitaries, are invited to stay in this special room.

The famed Lincoln Bedroom is also on this floor of the White House. Although President Lincoln never actually slept in this room, he did sign the Emancipation Proclamation here, on January 1, 1863. This controversial and powerful document gave nearly three million African-American slaves their freedom. An inspirational painting of slaves anticipating their freedom hangs in this room.

The Lincoln Bedroom contains a huge bed that Mary Todd Lincoln ordered. It is about 8 feet (2.4 m) long and nearly 6 feet (1.8 m) wide. The original mattress for this bed was made of horsehair. President Lincoln was a tall man, but it is believed that he never slept in the oversized bed. It was just one of many things the first lady ordered for the White House.

LINCOLN'S OVERSIZED BED IS PROBABLY THE BEST-KNOWN PIECE OF FURNITURE IN ALL OF THE WHITE HOUSE.

At that time, Congress gave each new president $20,000 to furnish and repair the White House. After redecorating the East Room in 1861, Mary Todd Lincoln purchased the rosewood bedroom furniture and overspent her given budget, infuriating her husband. He said to her, "It would stink in the nostrils of the American people to have it said that the President of the United States had approved a bill overrunning an appropriation of $20,000 for flub-dubs for this damned old house, when the soldiers cannot have blankets." Unfortunately for her, President Lincoln's wife was not a well-liked first lady. She was called greedy, vain, stupid, and wasteful. People thought she spent far too much money on furnishings and clothing. It is interesting that the furniture she bought turned out to be a famous and cherished part of this honored room.

It has been said that presidents Theodore Roosevelt and Dwight D. Eisenhower sensed a ghost of Abraham Lincoln in the Lincoln Bedroom. They both claimed to feel the powerful presence of President Lincoln in this room. Amy Carter, daughter of Jimmy Carter (who served 1977–81), often held sleepovers in this bedroom, and she and her friends would stay up to wait for the ghost of Lincoln to appear. During Ronald Reagan's administration (1981–89), Reagan's dog would bark outside this room, but never enter. However, President George Bush's dog, Millie, would go right into the room and hide rawhide bones, seemingly unfazed by any "ghost."

The Treaty Room, also on the second floor of the White House, got its name during President Kennedy's administration. Many significant decisions were made and treaties signed in this room throughout the years. President Kennedy signed a treaty for a Partial Nuclear Test Ban on October 7, 1963, and President Nixon signed a treaty on the Limitation of Antiballistic Missile Systems on September 30, 1972. When treaties are not being signed, this room is used for private meetings.

THIRD FLOOR OF THE WHITE HOUSE

The attic of the White House became a third floor in the renovation that took place during the administration of Calvin Coolidge. Fourteen rooms in all, including guest rooms, laundry and ironing rooms, servants' rooms, storage rooms, and a solarium, or sunroom, are located on the roof of the South Portico. First lady Jacqueline Kennedy used the solarium for a playgroup for her daughter, Caroline. When Caroline turned five years old, her mother set up a kindergarten class for her and several of her friends. The children received quite an edu-

CAROLINE KENNEDY, LEFT, WENT TO SCHOOL WITHOUT LEAVING HOME.
SHE ATTENDED KINDERGARTEN IN THE WHITE HOUSE SOLARIUM.

cation. In addition to their schoolwork, they got to meet famous visitors to the White House, went on tours to Washington museums, and saw movies in the White House theater. Often, President Kennedy went up to the third floor to visit his daughter and her classmates.

The solarium was first lady Rosalynn Carter's favorite room in the White House. Filled with bright sunshine, this room was the place where she often entertained friends.

THE OVAL OFFICE

The presidential Oval Office is not located in the main building, but in the West Wing, which slants off from the main building. Named for its shape and built in 1909 under the presidency of William Howard Taft, the Oval Office was moved twenty-five years later from the middle of the West Wing to its present location in the southeast corner. One of four oval rooms in the White House, the Oval Office is where the president meets formally with foreign leaders. Some of the president's most formal speeches are given and televised in this office.

Each president chooses the way in which the office is decorated. No matter what furniture or paintings are chosen, two items remain in place behind the desk for every president: the American flag, located to the right of the president, and the Presidential flag, standing to the left of the president.

PRESIDENTS USUALLY MAKE THEIR TELEVISED SPEECHES TO THE NATION FROM THE OVAL OFFICE.

THE RENOVATIONS DONE ON THE WHITE HOUSE DURING HARRY S. TRUMAN'S ADMINISTRATION WERE EXTENSIVE.

Chapter Five

WHITE HOUSE RENOVATIONS

A house as large and old as the White House needs constant renovations. Living in the White House has not always been glamorous, especially in the early years. Presidential families have had to cope with repairs, additions, and installations of such modern conveniences as running water and electricity. At times, because of repairs to the White House, some presidential families have been forced to live elsewhere.

The biggest repairs to the White House were done during Harry S. Truman's term. The house was in poor shape. Floors sagged, rooms were unsafe for use, and finally, the leg of a piano sank through a floor. The Trumans moved across the street to Blair House, a government guest house, in November 1948 and were not able to move back in until March 1952.

During the renovation, the entire house was gutted. Only the outer walls stood. Pictures of the inside, which was supported by steel frames, were not made public because the construction was such a mess. The layout of the White House remained essentially the same, as did the sizes of most rooms. The Ground Floor rooms included a large kitchen, the library, the oval Diplomatic

Reception Room (which is below the Blue Room), the Map Room, the Vermeil Room, and the China Room, with its display of former presidents' dinnerware. On the State Floor, the only big change was the large staircase, which was made wider and less steep and led down to the Entrance Hall.

Upstairs in the family quarters, more closet space was added and more bathrooms installed. Other than these changes, the rooms remained the same. After the work was completed, the White House contained 132 rooms. It grew as the country grew. By this time, the United States had forty-eight states.

Also during Harry S. Truman's term, a balcony was constructed on the second story behind the large columns. Known as the Truman Balcony because it was built at his suggestion, it was the first change to the outside of the White House since 1902. After the balcony was completed, another change had to be made—on the backs of twenty-dollar bills. These bills have a picture of the south side of the White House and had to be redesigned to include the new balcony.

In 1961, Jacqueline Kennedy decided to restore the inside of the White House to its original appearance. She appointed a Fine Arts Committee to help her. Many pieces of furniture and art objects were found and restored.

IN 1962, FIRST LADY JACQUELINE KENNEDY WELCOMED
A TELEVISION CREW INTO THE WHITE HOUSE TO TAPE A TOUR
OF THE RESTORED INTERIOR.

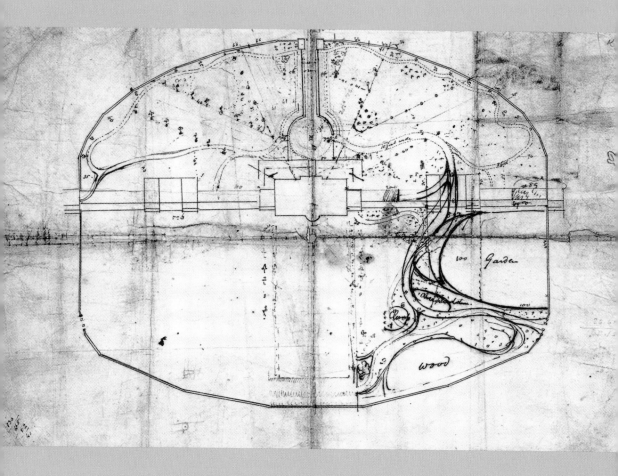

BENJAMIN HENRY LATROBE'S 1807 SKETCH OF THE WHITE HOUSE
GROUNDS SHOWS THE MIX OF GARDEN, WOODS, AND
OPEN SPACE ON THE SOUTH LAWN.

Chapter Six

THE PRESIDENT'S PARK

*B*efore Thomas Jefferson took office in 1801, the grounds of the President's House were in ruins. Piles of trash, tools, workmen's shacks, and rubble from construction were strewed all over. It was Jefferson who ordered improvements to the land around the President's House and dubbed it the President's Park. Jefferson made the south lawns for the president's private use and the north lawns for public use. He had grass mounds built on the South Lawn to assure some privacy on the east and west sides from the public.

John Adams's wife, Abigail Adams, thought the entire plot of land a vast expanse of wilderness. The land to the south of the President's House was marshy; the creek that ran by it was full of malaria-carrying mosquitoes. In 1817, the creek had been made into a canal, which contained garbage, dead animals, and pesky insects. The odor in the summertime heat was more than residents could stand. Finally, in 1872, the disease-bearing canal was filled in, covered, and made into a street called Constitution Avenue.

The sixth U.S. president, John Quincy Adams (who served 1825–29), son of the second president, John Adams, planted all types of trees and shrubs around the

White House. When he returned home from a trip, he always brought back seeds to plant at the White House. An elm tree that he planted on the South Lawn still stands today, and saplings from that tree are being saved for when the old tree needs to be replaced. Adams appeared to take more pleasure in gardening than he did in being president. He called his term of office the "four most miserable years of my life."

Andrew Jackson defeated John Quincy Adams in his bid for reelection in 1828. Born in South Carolina to poor parents, Jackson, unlike the first six wealthy presidents, truly represented the common people. Everyone was welcome at what he called "The People's House." He had James Hoban finish the North Portico and he decorated the East Room. President Jackson also planted a magnolia tree next to the South Portico in memory of his wife Rachel, who died a few weeks after his election. This beautiful magnolia stands there still.

During Jackson's administration, gravel walkways, a driveway to the north entrance of the house, a carriage house, and new stables were installed. In 1837, Jackson threw a huge party to celebrate George Washington's birthday and invited throngs of guests. A 1,400-pound (635-kg) cheese—4 feet (1.2 m) long and 2 feet (61 cm) wide—was put in the Entrance Hall. After the party, cheese lay everywhere in the White House and smelled for weeks. It was during the Jackson era that the White House got running water.

Harriet Lane, the niece and official hostess of the fifteenth U.S. president, James Buchanan, convinced her uncle to build a greenhouse on the White House lawns. This greenhouse, or conservatory, remained until the West Wing was built, when it was torn down.

The grounds around the White House originally numbered 60 acres (24 ha). Today, the White House stands on 18 acres (7 ha) of land. The Rose Garden,

CRAB-APPLE TREES AND TULIPS FLOWER IN THE ROSE GARDEN, ON THE WEST SIDE OF THE WHITE HOUSE. PRESIDENTIAL RECEPTIONS AND STATE DINNERS ARE SOMETIMES HELD HERE.

located near the Oval Office, is probably the most famous of all the White House gardens. Tricia Nixon, daughter of Richard M. Nixon, was the first daughter of a president to be married outside at the White House. She chose the Rose Garden for her ceremony, which took place on June 12, 1971.

THE EASTER EGG ROLL IS A POPULAR WHITE HOUSE TRADITION THAT DATES ALL THE WAY BACK TO DOLLEY MADISON.

After his resignation on August 9, 1974, President Nixon and his wife bid an emotional farewell on the South Lawn to members of the White House staff and boarded a waiting helicopter and took off. President Nixon was the only U.S. president ever to resign.

There are two "secret" gardens on the lawns of the White House. The first is the Children's Garden, which was presented to the White House as a Christmas gift from President Lyndon B. Johnson (who served 1963–69) and his wife. Names, handprints, and footprints of White House grandchildren have been engraved in bronze and put into the flagstones. There is a tiny water-lily pond in this garden. Almost hidden by the holly trees that line its path, this garden is a favorite among White House grandchildren. George and Barbara Bush, at the time of their stay at the White House (1989–93), had twelve grandchildren who were all delighted with this secret place.

The second secret garden was put in place during Ronald Reagan's administration. This garden, located right outside the Oval Office, is a haven for presidents in office.

Each year the White House organizes an Easter Egg Roll on the South Lawn for children on Easter Monday. Dolley Madison started this tradition. In the 1993 egg hunt, children looked for wooden eggs stamped with a picture of the White House and Bill and Hillary Clinton's signatures.

Chapter Seven

PRESENTIAL RECREATION

Living in the White House might sound appealing, but it is far from carefree. The first family does not enjoy the privacy of average American families. Because the job is filled with enormous responsibilities and difficult decisions, presidents need to have some fun and relaxation. Each president has relaxed in different ways.

Richard M. Nixon loved to bowl and had a single-lane bowling alley put in under the driveway near the North Portico. His best game was a 233, which is a presidential best. Sometimes he would bowl twenty games in one night!

Other presidents have loved swimming. Since the days of Franklin D. Roosevelt, the White House has had a pool. Roosevelt's pool cost about $40,000 to build. People donated the money, including pennies collected from children. Other presidents who enjoyed the White House pool were Truman, Eisenhower, Kennedy, Johnson, and Ford. During Nixon's administration, however, the pool was covered up, and the area was used for the press. When Ford came into office, workers built an outdoor pool.

Other recreational facilities at the White House include tennis courts, horseshoes, an exercise gym, bil-

IT IS DIFFICULT FOR PRESIDENTS TO ESCAPE THE LIMELIGHT. HERE,
PRESIDENT GERALD FORD SWIMS A LAP FOR THE PRESS.

liard tables, a movie theater, and a putting green. Each
president likes different kinds of recreation, and these
preferences are usually accommodated.

THE COCKPIT OF A SMALL SINGLE-ENGINE PLANE LIES AGAINST THE SOUTH WALL OF THE WHITE HOUSE AFTER HITTING THE LAWN AND SLIDING INTO THE BUILDING ON SEPTEMBER 12, 1994.

Chapter Eight

SECURITY AT THE WHITE HOUSE

The White House and the presidential family are protected by Secret Service agents. The Secret Service, an agency of the U.S. Department of the Treasury, was established on July 5, 1865. These agents are highly trained and skilled, but there have been times when intruders have nearly succeeded in doing damage to the White House.

An army maintenance mechanic crashed his helicopter on the South Lawn in 1974. In 1976 alone, there were six incidents where people tried to invade the grounds at the White House. Gerald Ford was president at the time. Four people at four different times tried to climb the fence to gain entry; a man left a briefcase at the main gate (officials feared a bomb was in it, but none was found); and another man drove his truck into the steel barrier that surrounds the White House.

On September 12, 1994, at 1:49 A.M., a mentally disturbed thirty-eight-year-old man from Maryland named Frank Eugene Corder crashed a stolen single-engine Cessna plane into the South Lawn. Part of the plane came very close to the south wall of the White House, just two stories below Bill and Hillary Clinton's bedroom. Fortunately, the Clintons were not at the White House. They were staying across the street at Blair House while renovations were being done. The crash caused minor damage. The magnolia tree that Andrew Jackson had planted in memory of his wife long ago was clipped, and a stone wall was damaged. The pilot of the stolen plane was killed in the crash.

Several hours after the incident, President Clinton reassured people that the White House would remain open to Americans. He said, "We take this incident seriously because the White House is the people's house and it is the job of every president who lives here to keep it safe and secure. So let me assure all Americans, the people's house will be kept safe, it will be kept open, and the people's business will go on."

Only months later, President Clinton announced that Pennsylvania Avenue would close to all motor vehicles for a two-block stretch in front of the White House. It was a historic decision. Since John and Abigail Adams first took up residence in the President's House in 1800, horses, trolleys, cars, and buses passed by 1600 Pennsylvania Avenue without restriction. However, after the bombing of a federal office building in Oklahoma City, Oklahoma, on April 19, 1995, security was tightened in federal buildings across the country, including the White House. Since May 20, 1995, the only traffic in front of the White House has been pedestrians.

Over the years, the White House has been many things: the president's home and office, a historical landmark, an architectural showpiece, and a national museum. First and foremost, this building has stood as a house of the people.

SOUTH PORTICO OF THE WHITE HOUSE

Visiting the White House

Over 1.5 million visitors toured the White House during Bill Clinton's first year of office, in 1993. That's about 30,000 people per week (Tuesday through Saturday) who go through the public rooms of the White House.

Tickets can be obtained by waiting in line at a ticket booth on the Ellipse, south of the White House. The lines can be long, and visitors must get there early in the morning. People sometimes line up as early as 5:00 A.M. These tickets are free of charge, but only about 5,500 are given out a day. The self-guided tours are scheduled between 10:00 A.M. and noon and last between twenty and thirty-five minutes.

Another way to get tickets for a tour of the White House is by writing a local member of Congress in advance. Each congressional office receives tickets for tours that are guided by Secret Service agents, who provide interesting facts about White House history. These tours are also free.

For current information about visiting the White House, call the White House Visitors Office Tour Line at (202) 456-7041.

For Further Reading

About the White House, U.S. Presidents, and Washington, D.C.

Fisher, Leonard E. *White House.* New York: Holiday House, 1989.

Hilton, Suzanne. *A Capital Capital City, 1790–1814.* New York: Atheneum, 1992.

Marsh, Carole. *Yes, You Have to Wipe Your Feet: White House Trivia.* Atlanta, Ga.: Gallopade Publishing Group, 1994.

Rubel, David. *The Scholastic Encyclopedia of the Presidents and Their Times.* New York: Scholastic, 1994.

Sullivan, George. *How the White House Really Works.* New York: Scholastic, 1990.

Waters, Kate. *The Story of the White House.* New York: Scholastic, 1991.

About Visiting Washington, D.C.

Munro, Roxie. *The Inside-Outside Book of Washington, D.C.* New York: Puffin Books, 1993.

Pedersen, Anne. *Kidding Around Washington, D.C., A Young Person's Guide.* Sante Fe, N. Mex.: John Muir Publications, 1993.

Weston, Marti, and Florri Decell. *Washington! Adventure for Kids.* Arlington, Va.: Vandamere Press, 1990.

Resources on the Internet

- To send an E-mail message to the president or vice-president of the United States, use the following addresses:

  president@whitehouse.gov

  vice.president@whitehouse.gov

- The White House has its own World Wide Web page that offers virtual tours, historical information, and even an audible welcome message from the president. To reach this site, use the following address:

  http://www.whitehouse.gov

- The California Institute of Technology maintains an anonymous ftp archive of White House press releases, speeches, and other materials. Connect to their archive at the following address:

  ftp.cco.caltech.edu

Index

About the Author

Patricia Ryon Quiri lives in Palm Harbor, Florida, with her husband and three sons. She has an elementary education degree from Alfred University in New York and teaches second grade in the Pinellas County school system. Other Franklin Watts books by Ms. Quiri include *Metamorphosis, The Algonquians,* and *Dolley Madison.*